WACKY and WILD!

GUINNESS WORLD RECORDS

WACKY and WILD!

GUINNESS WORLD RECORDS

by CALISTA BRILL

HARPER

An Imprint of HarperCollinsPublishers

GUINNESS WORLD RECORDS: OFFICIALLY AMAZING

Since 1955, Guinness World Records has been the world's most trusted, accurate, and recognized source for record-breaking achievements. From a dog who rides a scooter to the longest line of carved pumpkins to the most fire hoops spun, Guinness World Records is home to wacky, gross, and wild record holders, including the Officially Amazing feats in this book!

Guinness World Records holders are truly amazing, but all attempts to set or break records are performed under controlled conditions and at the participant's own risk. Please seek out the appropriate guidance before you attempt any record-breaking activities.

Guinness World Records: Wacky and Wild!
© 2016 Guinness World Records Limited
The words GUINNESS WORLD RECORDS and related logos are
trademarks of Guinness World Records Limited.
All records and information accurate as of September 1, 2015.
All rights reserved. Printed in the United States of America.
No part of this book may be used or reproduced in any manner
whatsoever without written permission except in the case of brief
quotations embodied in critical articles and reviews. For information
address HarperCollins Children's Books, a division of HarperCollins
Publishers, 195 Broadway, New York, NY 10007.
www.harpercollinschildrens.com

Library of Congress Control Number: 2015955156
ISBN 978-0-06-234176-1

Design by Victor Joseph Ochoa and Sean Boggs
15 16 17 18 19   PC/RRDC   10 9 8 7 6 5 4 3 2 1
❖
First Edition

SECTION ONE:
ANIMALS

BowWOW! The natural world is a crazy place. From the planet's largest spider to the smallest horse, our buddies in the animal kingdom are just full of surprises!

Some people live with a dog or a cat or a pet bird. Not many people live with scorpions, especially not on purpose! Kanchana Ketkaew of Thailand lived in a small glass room containing 5,320 scorpions from December 22, 2008, to January 24, 2009. That's the **longest duration living with scorpions**! During her 33 days in the room, Ketkaew was stung 13 times—and lived to tell the tale!

ONE HECK OF A HAIRBALL

The **heaviest ball of dog hair** weighed 201 pounds. That's heavier than a lot of grown-up people! The ball was created by Texas Hearing and Service Dogs in Austin, Texas, on April 7, 2012. The hairball included hair shed by 8,126 dogs!

POP STAR

Cally the Wonderdog really lives up to her name—just don't invite her to your birthday party if you want to keep your balloons! Not fazed by being on a live television show, Cally and her owner, Mitch Jenkins, from the UK, achieved the **fastest time to pop 100 balloons by a dog**—41.67 seconds on May 25, 2015. Cally later visited the head office of Guinness World Records in London, UK, to show off her skill and to receive her very own official certificate.

Speaking of dogs, how would you like a hot dog? What about a hot dog that weighs over 7 pounds? That's bigger than some *real* dogs! Gorilla Tango Novelty Meats set the record for the **longest hot dog commercially available** on March 21, 2011. It measures 16 inches long and 4 inches in diameter and costs $40.

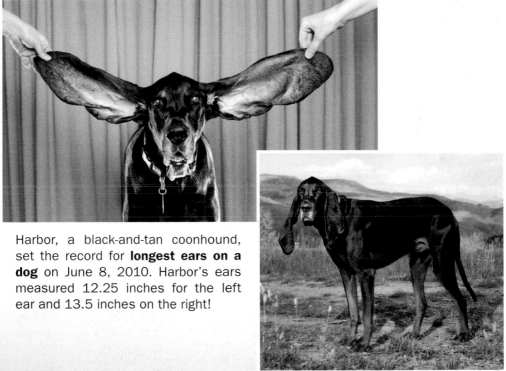

Harbor, a black-and-tan coonhound, set the record for **longest ears on a dog** on June 8, 2010. Harbor's ears measured 12.25 inches for the left ear and 13.5 inches on the right!

If you like dogs—and Halloween—then this must be your dream parade! On July 27, 2011, 337 dressed-up dogs set the world record for the **most dogs in a costume parade**. The dogs walked a distance of 1,104 feet around the Petco Park baseball field in San Diego, California, right before a baseball game (San Diego Padres vs. Arizona Diamondbacks).

On December 9, 2012, a world record was set in Hong Kong: the **most people brushing dogs' teeth simultaneously**. Have you ever tried to brush a dog's teeth? It's hard enough getting one dog to cooperate . . . let alone 268 of them! No wonder this is a world record!

THE NOT-SO-ITSY-BITSY SPIDER

The world's **largest spider** is the male goliath bird-eating spider (*Theraphosa blondi*). This particular spider was collected by the Pablo San Martin Expedition at Rio Cavro, Venezuela, in April 1965. The record-setting spider had a leg span of 11 inches—big enough to cover a dinner plate.

The goliath bird-eating spiders are a species of tarantula. They are mostly found in the coastal rain forests of Suriname, Guyana, and French Guiana, but a few of them have been found in Venezuela and Brazil.

Although the goliath bird-eating spider may occasionally take young birds from their nests, it is much more likely to feed on rodents and amphibians, such as rats and frogs. It kills its prey with the force of its huge fangs and its venom, which is not harmful to humans. It also has dangerous hairs all over its body. It can flick these hairs at anyone it sees as a threat, and they cause an extremely itchy rash.

Colo is the **oldest living gorilla in captivity** and also the **first gorilla born in captivity**. Born in 1956, the popular resident at Columbus Zoo in Powell, Ohio, was 58 years, 214 days, as of July 23, 2015. She attained the title following the death on September 4, 2008, of Jenny, a western lowland gorilla at Dallas Zoo in Texas, whose age of 55 had been confirmed by the International Species Information System.

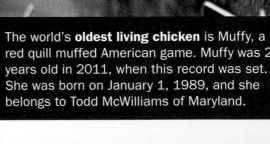

The world's **oldest living chicken** is Muffy, a red quill muffed American game. Muffy was 22 years old in 2011, when this record was set. She was born on January 1, 1989, and she belongs to Todd McWilliams of Maryland.

NOTHING BUT NET!

Zac the macaw loves basketball! He made 22 slam dunks in just one minute on December 31, 2011—that's the **most slam dunks by a parrot in one minute**. And that's not all this macaw can manage! Zac also holds the record for the **most canned drinks opened by a parrot in one minute**—35!

The **longest snake to ever live in captivity** is Medusa. She's a reticulated python. When she was measured on October 12, 2011, she was over 25 feet long! That's as long as two cars parked end to end.

SECTION ONE: *ANIMALS* **15**

The **tallest domestic cat ever** was named Savannah Islands Trouble. This towering feline was called "Trouble" by his owner, Debby Maraspini. On October 30, 2011, at the Silver Cats Cat Show, Trouble was measured at 19 inches tall. That's almost as tall as a Labrador retriever! Sadly, Trouble died on August 15, 2012.

GIANT JAKE!

Big Jake is the **tallest living horse**. Big Jake is a Belgian—a breed known for their size—and on January 19, 2010, he was measured at 20 hands, 2.75 inches. That's almost 7 feet tall! Big Jake lives on Smokey Hollow Farms in Poynette, Wisconsin, with owner Jerry Gilbert. In his spare time, he supports the Ronald McDonald House, brightening the days of families whose children are undergoing treatment at a nearby hospital.

HARK! HARK! THE DOGS DO BARK!

Most dogs can bark pretty loudly, but the **loudest bark** anyone has ever measured belongs to a golden retriever named Charlie. On October 20, 2012, Charlie barked so loudly that he set a new world record! His woof was measured at 113.1 decibels (dB). That's louder than most car horns!

What would you guess the **longest insect** would be? Maybe a centipede? Or a dragonfly? Not even close! The longest insect is the *Phobaeticus serratipes,* which is a stick insect that lives in Malaysia. This long fellow has a total length of 21 inches, including its legs. The length of its body alone is 11 inches!

Could you fit even one tennis ball in your mouth? No way, right? But Augie, a golden retriever owned by the Miller family in Texas, managed to hold five balls in his mouth at one time! He gathered and held all five tennis balls on July 6, 2003—setting the record for the **most tennis balls held in the mouth by a dog**.

Meet JJS Summer Breeze, a world-record-holding horse! This mare, hailing from Augusta, Kansas, has the **longest tail on a horse** in the entire world. Her tail measures 12 feet, 6 inches. . . . That's as long as a small car!

Sweet Pea is an Australian shepherd–border collie mix. This adorable dog set the record for **fastest 100 meters** (328 feet) **with a can balanced on the head by a dog**. She did it in just 2 minutes, 55 seconds in 2008. Sweet Pea is one level-headed pooch. She also holds the record for **most steps climbed balancing a glass of water on the head**: 17!

FOCUS ON: STRIKER!

Have you ever been in an old car with roll-down windows? It takes a while to turn that handle around enough to get the window open. But Striker, a border collie from Hungary, didn't have any trouble achieving the **fastest car window opened by a dog**. Striker took 11.34 seconds to roll down a nonelectric car window on September 1, 2004, in Quebec City, Canada!

Striker used his paw and nose to push the handle around. He kept checking the window to see how far it had reached! The window was 16 inches high, and the handle was 5 inches long.

EAT UP!

Human beings have speed-eating contests, but what about animals? If there were a contest, the winner among all the mammals would be the star-nosed mole, the **fastest-eating mammal**. This mole's proper name is *Condylura cristata*, and, boy, can it eat fast.

Scientist Dr. Kenneth Catania studies star-nosed moles. He discovered that the time it takes one of these moles to grab something, eat it, and move on was around 230 milliseconds. Some moles could do this in as fast as 120 milliseconds—that's one tenth of a second!

Itty-bitty Milly is a Chihuahua owned by Vanesa Semler of Puerto Rico. On February 21, 2013, Milly was measured at 3.8 inches tall, making her the world's **shortest living dog**. Milly is about as tall as a grapefruit . . . but much sweeter!

There was love in the air on July 12, 2012. But these two lovebirds weren't birds at all— they were dogs! Chilly Pasternak and Baby Hope Diamond had a New York City wedding that was so expensive it set a world record for **most-expensive pet wedding**. The final bill came to $158,187.26. Baby and Chilly's big day doubled as a fund-raiser for the Humane Society of New York!

A person *can* actually hold this horse—she weighs about as much as a dog! On July 7, 2006, Thumbelina was 17.5 inches tall at the shoulder, making her the world's **smallest living horse**. Thumbelina is a miniature horse, and she lives with Kay and Paul Goessling in St. Louis, Missouri. Thumbelina was born on March 1, 2002. She met her record-breaking counterpart, Radar, who was formerly the **tallest horse**, in 2006 (below).

PURR-FECTLY HEARD

When Merlin is in a good mood, everyone knows about it. That's because his purr—which measured 67.8 dB on April 2, 2015—is louder than an air conditioner, earning him the record of **loudest purr by a domestic cat**. Owner Tracy Westwood from Torquay, UK, said: "When you're watching films you have to turn the TV up or put him out of the room. I can [even] hear him when I'm drying my hair."

SECTIO

TWO:

VEHICLES

Vrooooooom! Ever since the wheel was invented, people have been coming up with new kinds of vehicles. And Guinness World Records is here to discover the weirdest and wildest ones out there! From the world's fastest toilet to the smallest helicopter, there's plenty to know about things that go.

To most people, a tricycle is a plastic toy that you ride in the driveway when you're three years old. But Wouter van den Bosch, of the Netherlands, built a very different kind of tricycle. This trike weighs 1,650 pounds—almost one ton! It became a world record setter—the **heaviest rideable trike**—in May 2010.

If you think Wouter van den Bosch's one-ton tricycle is impressive, get a load of this! On November 23, 2007, Tilo and Wilfried Niebel of Germany built the **heaviest rideable motorcycle**, and it weighs 10,470 pounds!

www.harzer-bike-schmiede.de

The **loudest bicycle horn** is capable of producing a sound pressure level of 136.2 dB. Nicknamed the Hornster, it was developed by the Environmental Transport Association (UK), and was demonstrated by Yannick Read of the UK on February 13, 2013, in Weybridge, Surrey, UK. The Hornster was built to highlight the dangers that cyclists face on busy roads. It uses a modified freight-train horn, powered by a scuba diving tank.

The **heaviest limousine** in the world is the Midnight Rider. This 70-foot-long luxury car weighs 50,560 pounds! That's 25 tons, or about as much as 15 normal cars! Midnight Rider was designed by Michael Machado and Pamela Bartholomew in California and has been operating since 2004.

Martin Bacon of the UK set a record on February 19, 2013, when he got his coffee-fueled vehicle up to 65 miles per hour. That's freeway speed for the **fastest coffee-powered vehicle**! Those fumes must have smelled great.

WHEN YOU GOTTA GO, YOU GOTTA GO!

The **fastest toilet** in the world is the Bog Standard. This mobile bathroom has everything: a bathtub, a sink, and even a laundry hamper. Built by inventor Edd China of the UK, it sits on top of a motorcycle and sidecar, and it can travel up to 42.25 miles per hour.

If you wanted to ride on this plane, you'd have to be the size of an ant! The world's **smallest radio-controlled model aircraft** was built by John Wakefield of the UK in October 2010. Its wingspan is just 2.72 inches! The aircraft flew for 6 minutes, 56 seconds . . . and it weighed just 0.07 ounces!

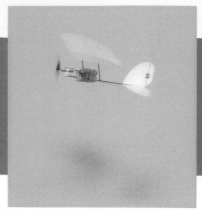

Most people find gardening very relaxing. But a garden shed zooming along at 58 miles per hour is the opposite of relaxing—it's exhilarating! Edd China built the **fastest garden shed** and revealed it to the world on the set of *Lo Show dei Record* in Italy on April 1, 2011. That's April Fool's Day . . . but this was no joke.

The **smallest helicopter** is the GEN H-4. This remarkable machine is made by the Gen Corporation of Japan. The length of its rotors is only 13 feet—giving it the smallest rotor length of any helicopter in the world. The GEN H-4 has one seat, one set of landing gear, and one power unit. It weighs only 154 pounds . . . about as much as a single passenger!

DIVE DEEP!

Submarines are not usually very roomy. But the **smallest submarine** is a *really* tight fit. It was made by Pierre Poulin of Canada, and its official dive was in the Memphremagog Lake of Magog, Quebec, on June 26, 2005. Poulin's submarine is called *BIG* and can turn in a full circle. It can also go up and down through the water without help. Poulin piloted the sub and stayed 16 feet underwater inside it for 43 minutes.

TRUCKASAURUS!

The **largest mining truck** is the monstrous Belaz 75710 with a volume of 22,792 cubic feet. It was made by construction vehicle manufacturer Belaz of Belarus and tested at their premises on January 22, 2014. The giant earthmover can carry 450 tons at once, which means it also takes the record for **highest rated payload capacity**. The truck was built as part of the general trend within the mining industry for increasing the unit sizes of machinery, to make them capable of moving greater loads per haul cycle.

SECTION THREE:

COLLECTIONS

Spoons . . . Baseball cards . . . Toothpaste tubes?! Do you have any collections? Maybe you collect stickers or cards or interesting rocks? Most people collect a few things . . . but there are some people who have set world records for their extraordinary collections!

HELLO, KITTY!

Asako Kanda lives in Japan along with her 4,519 different Hello Kitty items. She became a world record holder of the **largest collection of Hello Kitty memorabilia** on August 14, 2011. Kanda's house is stuffed full of Hello Kitty items, including everything from a Hello Kitty frying pan to a Hello Kitty electric fan, and even a Hello Kitty toilet seat!

Wendy Suen of China loves snow globes. Her collection is the largest in the world—as of April 7, 2008, she had 1,888, the **largest collection of snow globes**. She's been collecting snow globes since 2000.

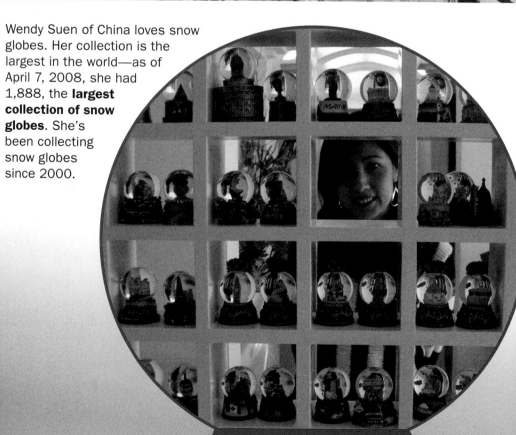

Joshua Mueller is the proud owner of the **largest collection of Converse shoes**. His collection in Lakewood, Washington, had grown to 1,546 pairs of Converse shoes when it was counted on March 8, 2012. Mueller doesn't just collect Converse shoes. He also wears them! But he has so many that he could wear a different pair every day for over four years without repeating. He's careful to keep all his shoes clean and looking their best. He even wears plastic bags over the Converse shoes whenever he has to walk somewhere dirty.

PEARLY WHITES!

The **largest collection of toothpaste tubes** belongs to dentist Val Kolpakov of Georgia (USA). Guess how many tubes of toothpaste he has? 2,037! Kolpakov's collection has tubes from all over the world—including Japan, Korea, China, India, and Russia. The rarest item in his collection dates from a time before toothpaste had even been invented: an English silver toothpowder box from 1801.

Betty Davis of Yucaipa, California, sure loves beavers—so much that she has been collecting them for more than 35 years! She has the **largest collection of beavers** in the world—a record that was verified on December 15, 2011. Davis has 608 individual beaver items in her collection!

Collecting candy sounds like fun, right? Then you get to eat it! But what about just collecting the wrappers? That's exactly what Amanda Destro of Venice, Italy, has been doing. On February 16, 2012, she had 2,048 candy wrappers! She had bccn amassing the **largest collection of candy wrappers** for 22 years. Destro started out using the wrappers as bookmarks while she was studying. Her collection features wrappers from all over the world! That includes Poland, Slovakia, Chile, Peru, and Panama.

Lots of girls have a Barbie doll or two . . . but Bettina Dorfmann of Germany has 15,000 of them—the **largest collection of Barbie dolls**! She set the world record in October 2011, but she's been collecting Barbies since 1993. That's a big bunch of Barbies!

770. That's how many different chocolate bars Bob Brown owned as of October 29, 2010, when he became the world record holder of the **largest collection of chocolate bars**. Brown's delicious collection lines the walls of his basement when it's not on display in public.

In 1952, Carol McFadden began collecting earrings. Known as the Earring Lady, her collection featured 37,706 pairs as of 2006, making it the **largest collection of earrings**. According to Carol, the most unusual earrings she owns is a set of toilets made from turquoise and white plastic!

SECTION FOUR:

FOOD & DRINK

Hope you're hungry! Have you ever been in a pie-eating contest? Have you ever seen a pumpkin that weighs more than you do? That stuff is small potatoes compared to some of the wild food records people have set over the years. Let Guinness World Records be your guide through the world of unbelievable food and drink!

The **largest coiled sausage** had a 13-foot diameter and weighed about 750 pounds before it was cooked. It was created by Udruženje Kobasicijada in Turija, Serbia, on February 23, 2013.

Even the hungriest bagel fan might be a little overwhelmed by this one. The **largest bagel** weighed 868 pounds and was made by Bruegger's Bagels. If you were at the Great New York State Fair on August 27, 2004, you could have seen it in person!

TOOT TOOT TOOT ON YOUR CARROT FLUTE!

It's pretty surprising that there's one person in the world who plays an instrument made out of a vegetable. It's even crazier that there's an entire orchestra full of people playing different vegetable instruments! The Vegetable Orchestra of Austria holds the world record for the **most concerts performed by a vegetable orchestra**. Guess how many concerts they played between April 1998 and September 2012? 77!

Regular watermelons are already really heavy. Just imagine trying to carry the **heaviest watermelon**. At 350 pounds, 8 ounces, this fruit weighed as much as the average gorilla! This monster melon was grown by Chris Kent of Tennessee in 2013.

Fancy a picnic with several hundred of your best friends? You'll all fit just fine on the **largest picnic blanket**, which covers an area of 18,944 square feet! This blanket was woven at the Melin Tregwynt Mill in Wales, UK, for supermarket chain Waitrose Ltd. It was laid out for the first time in Durban, South Africa, in April 2008.

DON'T STRING ME ALONG!

The **longest onion string** measured 3.6 miles and was made by 33 people. The onion string was created for the Turda Fest Festival in Romania in 2008. It would take you an entire hour to walk the length of that onion string, and that's if you were walking fast!

Just imagine the mess when the **largest snow cone** melted! This monster weighed 25,080 pounds. It was created by Bahama Buck's Original Shaved Ice Company in Texas on December 10, 2011. The flavor of the world's largest snow cone was birthday cake. Yum!

The **largest cookie** baked was made by the Immaculate Baking Company in Flat Rock, North Carolina. The record-setting chocolate-chip cookie measured 8,120 square feet and weighed 40,000 pounds! It had a diameter of 101 feet.

Everybody likes a good baked potato, but how do you feel about 3,784 pounds and 7 ounces of them? A little much, right? Not for Guinness World Records! The **largest serving of baked potatoes** was a batch of *huatiada* cooked by the Comité Organizador de Fegasur in Juliaca, Peru, on June 9, 2012.

FACT!

Huatiada is a traditional potato dish from Peru. It's made by baking the potatoes in an earth oven, then burying the oven—and the potatoes. Cooking for this record-setting batch of potatoes took around 90 minutes. This dish is often accompanied by cheese.

FLIPPING AMAZING!

If you've ever tried to flip a pancake, you know it can be tricky. One false move, and there's a pancake on your floor or ceiling! But Dominic Cuzzacrea doesn't have any trouble catching pancakes. He flipped one a staggering 31 feet, 1 inch in the air, on November 13, 2010, in Cheektowaga, New York. This broke his own previous record for the **highest pancake toss** by almost a foot!

There aren't a lot of folks in the world making sculptures out of bread, and most of them aren't making 10-foot-tall bread sculptures. But Ciril Hitz, Mitch Stamm, and Robert Zielinski set a world record for **tallest bread sculpture** on February 6, 2010. Their statue was more than 18 feet tall!

THIS CAKE IS FOR THE DOGS!

In celebration of the UK's royal wedding on April 15, 2011, a corgi-themed dog cake was created on that day. The **largest cake for dogs** was made by professional cake maker Michelle Wibowo and weighed in at 150 pounds! It featured a giant corgi made of frosting on the top in honor of the queen's famous pets.

The record for the **most candles on a cake** is 48,523 and was set by Ashrita Furman in conjunction with members of the Sri Chinmoy Centre in New York on August 27, 2008. That's one way to celebrate a birthday!

The **largest wedding cake** was made for a bridal showcase. But can you imagine being at a wedding with a cake that weighed 15,032 pounds? It would take a whole lot of guests to eat all that cake! This record-setting wedding cake was made by the chefs at the Mohegan Sun Hotel and Casino on February 8, 2004.

SANTA CLAUS IS COMING TO TOWN!

A chocolate Santa is a nice holiday treat! But what do you do with the **tallest chocolate Santa Claus** that stands 16 feet, 5 inches tall? It's going to take a long time to eat your way through that one! This record-setting Santa was unveiled in Mirabello, Italy, on December 11, 2011.

The **longest cotton candy** was 4,593 feet, 2 inches! That's almost a mile long! It was created by Kocaeli Fuar Müdürlügü in Izmit, Kocaeli, Turkey, on July 10, 2009. Imagine starting at one end and eating your way to the other! It might take you quite a while!

BUSY BAKER!

How many cupcakes can fit in your oven? Maybe 12? Or 24? You'd need a much bigger oven—or a whole lot of regular-size ones—to beat this record! The **most cupcakes baked in one hour** is 1,260. This impressive baking feat was achieved by N1 City Mall and Francor Bakery in South Africa on October 27, 2011. Do you think all those cupcakes got eaten up in an hour, too?

Fish sticks are also called fish fingers. That's because they're about the same size as someone's finger. Well, not this one. The **largest fish stick** was 6 feet, 6 inches long, 1 foot, 7 inches wide, 5.7 inches high, and weighed close to 300 pounds. It was made by Michael Gorich in Bremerhaven, Germany. This record was set on January 22, 2009.

Baked beans sure are tasty, no matter how you eat them. In 2011, Garry Eccles of the UK (pictured) ate 258—the **most beans eaten using a cocktail stick in five minutes**. This feat has since been beaten, though, by regular record-setter Ashrita Furman, who consumed 271 beans in 2014.

THE SWEETEST SCULPTURE!

People use lots of different materials for sculpture. Stone, wood, metal . . . even ice or butter. But it's not every day you see a chocolate sculpture this big. In fact, this is one of a kind . . . the **largest chocolate candy sculpture**! It weighed 589 pounds, 8 ounces and measured 5 feet long.

The chocolate candy sculpture was created by Namba Walk of Japan on February 10, 2012, and was heart-shaped for Valentine's Day. It was made with layers of marble chocolate and sugar solution mixed with vinegar.

Jelly is hard enough to eat with a spoon, but how about with chopsticks? In 2010, Ashrita Furman (pictured) got through 1 pound, 5 ounces to earn the record for **most jelly eaten with chopsticks in one minute**. This has since been beaten by Cherry Yoshitake of Japan, aka Mr. Cherry, who ate 1 pound, 6 ounces on July 9, 2014.

How many meatballs can *you* eat in one sitting? Five or six? Meet Takeru Kobayashi of Japan. On March 8, 2010, Kobayashi ate 29 meatballs in one minute, earning him the record for **most meatballs eaten in a minute**. He also holds records for speed-eating hot dogs and hamburgers. Burp!

I SCREAM, YOU SCREAM . . .

. . . we all scream, "That's so much ice cream!" The **largest ice-cream cake** weighed 22,333 pounds and was created by Dairy Queen in Toronto, Canada, on May 10, 2011. The cake was 14 feet, 6 inches long, 13 feet wide, and over 3 feet tall! It was made of sponge cake, vanilla ice cream, buttercream frosting, and Oreo cookie topping. Yum!

WHO DOESN'T LOVE A BIG SLICE OF PIE?

And we do mean *big*. Check out the **largest pumpkin pie**! It was made by New Bremen Giant Pumpkin Growers in Ohio on September 25, 2010. It weighed 3,699 pounds! This beat their own record by 1,679 pounds.

The **longest line of carved pumpkins** included a staggering 1,510 pumpkins and was achieved by FivePoint Communities at the Pumpkin Glow event held in Irvine, California, on October 25, 2014. Students from several local schools, as well as residents of Great Park Neighborhoods, worked together to make the record a success. Pumpkin sculptor Scott Gerber also demonstrated some live carving techniques at the event.

THIS WILL SCRAMBLE YOUR BRAINS!
How do you like your eggs in the morning? For this record, you were only ever going to get them one way. The **largest batch of scrambled eggs** was served up by wholesale and supply store Zakład Pakowania Jaj Mering of Poland, on July 26, 2014. Overall, 29,096 eggs were scrambled and the cooking time was 2 hours and 45 minutes.

The world's **heaviest lemon** weighed 11 pounds, 9.7 ounces on January 8, 2003. There hasn't been a heavier lemon in over 10 years! This colossal citrus fruit was grown by Aharon Shemoel of Israel on his farm. The lemon had a circumference of 29 inches and was 13 inches high.

Here's an exciting new skill to practice: throwing eggs into the air, then catching them in your mouth. It's tricky! But Ashrita Furman and Bipin Larkin are experts at it. They set the world record for **most eggs thrown and then caught in the mouth in one minute**, on November 15, 2012. They managed 12!

Sergio and Maria Socorro Bodiongan of the Philippines are the proud holders of the record for **heaviest mango**. Their monstrous mango weighed 7 pounds, 9.12 ounces on August 27, 2009.

What a cabbage! This giant of the vegetable kingdom weighed more than 138 pounds on August 31, 2012, when it was officially declared the **heaviest cabbage**. It was grown in Alaska.

APPLE OF MY EYE!

The **heaviest apple** weighed 4 pounds, 1 ounce on October 24, 2005. That's bigger than most cabbages! This awesome apple was grown and picked by Chisato Iwasaki at his apple farm in Hirosaki City, Japan.

Squish! The **heaviest squash** in the world weighs 1,486 pounds, 9.6 ounces—over half a ton!—and was grown by Joel Jarvis of Canada. This horse-size squash set the world record on October 1, 2011.

The **heaviest turnip** in the world weighed 39 pounds, 3 ounces and was grown by Scott and Mardie Robb, who presented it at the Alaska State Fair on September 1, 2004. The variety is appropriately called Mammoth Purple Top Turnip (*Brassica rupa*).

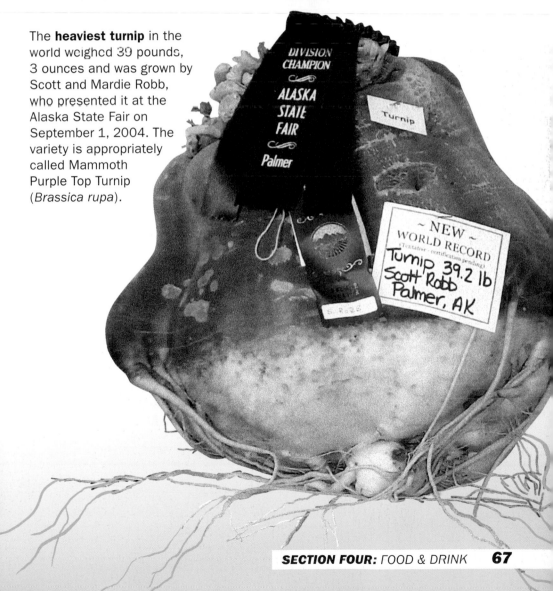

SECTION FIVE:

DON'T TRY THIS AT HOME!

Safety equipment not included! Lots of world records have an element of danger. For example, imagine if you collected thousands of chocolate bars and then they all fell on you! But the records in this section are some of the scariest, craziest, and just plain most dangerous stunts Guinness World Records has ever seen!

Don't even *think* about trying any of these at home . . . but aren't you glad these folks *did*?

N

The **most consecutive rope skips on a bed of nails over another person** is 117. Ouch! This cringe-inducing record was achieved by skipper Amy Bruney on a bed of nails balanced over her husband, Jon. They set the record on *Guinness World Records Unleashed* in Los Angeles, California, on June 25, 2013.

70

Breaking a concrete block is pretty impressive already. But breaking a concrete block on someone else with a sledgehammer is something else! Add a ticking clock to all that, and you've got a Guinness World Records feat: the **fastest time to break 16 concrete blocks on the body of a female**. Record holders Daniella D'Ville (aka Danielle Martin) and Johnny Strange (both from the UK) managed it in 30.4 seconds on October 12, 2013!

Smashing a coconut with your elbow isn't most people's idea of a good time. But Tae Kwon Do expert Edin Kajevic of Bosnia and Herzegovina demolished 40 to set the record for **most coconuts smashed by elbows in one minute** on November 30, 2014.

On February 29, 2012 (leap day!), martial arts specialist Keshab Swain of India smashed 85 *green* coconuts with his elbow in one minute. That's the **most green coconuts smashed by elbows in one minute**!

On November 16, 2013, at the age of 83, strongman Abdurakhman Abdulazizov of Russia wasn't ready for retirement. Instead he was setting a hair-raising record: the **greatest weight lifted with the hair**. Using just his locks, he picked up a scalp-stretching 179 pounds, 10.82 ounces, surpassing the previous mark by more than 36 pounds!

Here's a wacky record for you: the **most apples held in one's own mouth and cut by a chain saw in one minute**! Well, the number is eight, held by Johnny Strange, who achieved this terrifying feat on October 12, 2013.

IT'S A DOWNWARD SPIRAL!

The **longest metal coil passed through the nose and out of the mouth** measured 11 feet, 10.91 inches in length. It was achieved by Andrew Stanton on the set of *Lo Show dei Record* in Rome, Italy, on March 31, 2012.

"Fire torch teething" is a fire-eating act where you use your teeth to hold a flaming torch with no hands. It's not for amateurs! **The longest duration of fire torch teething** is 2 minutes, 1.51 seconds. The record is held by Carisa Hendrix of Canada, and she performed this amazing stunt on the set of *Lo Show dei Record* in Rome, Italy, on April 12, 2012.

How many swords can *you* swallow? How about while you're riding a unicycle? Well, Australian daredevil Chayne Hultgren managed to swallow three while atop the precarious ride, achieving the **most swords swallowed on a unicycle**. Nobody has bettered his record since 2012.

Chayne is better known as the Space Cowboy. That's a pretty good name for a guy who holds the world record for the **most chain saw– juggling catches on a unicycle**—eight catches! Juggling chain saws is scary enough already . . . kudos to the brave Space Cowboy for adding the unicycle to this terrifying mix!

The **most apples held in someone else's mouth and cut in half by chain saw in one minute** is 12. The record is held by Johnny Strange, who chain-sawed apples from the mouth of Daniella D'Ville at the Doncaster Tattoo Jam in South Yorkshire, UK, on October 12, 2013. Sometimes two heads are better than one!

The human jaw is incredibly strong! That's why Georges Christen of Luxembourg was able to carry a table more than 32 feet in 6.57 seconds . . . in his *mouth*. That's right: the record for **fastest 10 meters carrying a table and weight in the mouth** is held by Georges. He set this record on June 18, 2009.

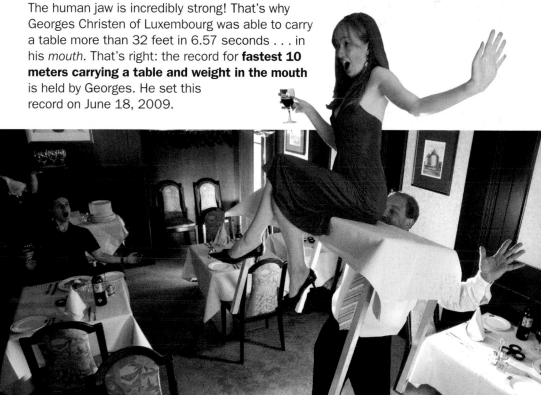

IT'S A JUGGLING ACT . . .

The Great Gordo Gamsby from Australia juggled three fire clubs while swallowing a sword on September 14, 2012. He kept the three clubs aloft for the requisite minimum of 10 seconds, making him the record holder for **most fire clubs juggled while sword-swallowing**!

DON'T FORGET TO FLUSH!

You have one minute. How many wooden toilet seats can *you* break using your head in that time? Probably not as many as Kevin Shelley, who broke 46 toilet seats with his head on September 1, 2007, achieving the **most toilet seats broken by the head in one minute**.

The **most torches extinguished with the mouth in 30 seconds** is . . . 39! This painful and impressive record was achieved by pyrotechnician Hubertus Wawra of Germany on the set of *Guinness World Records—Ab India Todega* in Mumbai, India, on February 21, 2011.

QUEEN OF SWORDS

The **most swords swallowed at the same time by a female** is 13, as achieved by Natasha Veruschka on September 3, 2004. Each of the swords was at least 15 inches long. Here she is pictured swallowing a neon sword—a 24-inch glass tube filled with neon gas!

The **most baking trays buckled over the head by a team of two in one minute** is 55 and was achieved by Canadian daredevil duo Burnaby Q. Orbax and Sweet Pepper Klopek (aka Monsters of Schlock). They achieved this record in Niagara, Ontario, Canada, on August 31, 2012. Bet they had sore heads the morning after!

Meet Pippa "The Ripper" Coram of Australia! She holds the record for **most fire hoops spun while in the splits position**! Coram managed to spin three burning Hula-Hoops at once while doing the splits on September 14, 2012. She kept the hot hoops spinning around her arms and neck for the required 10 seconds in order to set this record.

THAT'S SOME AIM!

The **most knives thrown backward around a human target in one minute** is 63! That's just over one knife thrown per second! This astonishing record was achieved by Patrick Brumbach of Germany on August 17, 2011, who was throwing the knives around his very trusting wife.

Feeling dizzy? You will be in a second. The **most rotations hanging from a power drill in one minute** is 148, set by The Huy Giang of Germany on December 2008. This bettered his own record by seven rotations!

The **fastest time to extract five nails from wood using teeth** is 7.44 seconds and was achieved by Steve Schmidt in Columbia, Missouri, on November 8, 2014. Steve is a fifth-generation farmer and world champion weightlifter. He used eastern white pine wood for the attempt, which has a Janka hardness rating of 380.

Casey Severn had to be pretty snappy to achieve the record for the **most mousetraps released on the tongue in one minute**—ouch! He managed to get through 53 traps on October 12, 2014, at the Maryland Renaissance Festival held in Crownsville, Maryland.

Let's get straight to the point with this one. On December 26, 2007, Target Girl Tiny Nagy had 102 14-inch throwing knives hurled at her in one minute by Dr. David R. Adamovich. David, better known as The Great Throwdini, broke the world record for **most knives thrown around a human target in one minute**.

The **fastest time to husk a coconut using the teeth** is 28.06 seconds! This record was achieved by Sidaraju S. Raju of India, who husked a coconut measuring 30.7 inches in circumference on March 30, 2003.

A REAL BACK-BREAKER

Matt Dopson really put his back into this record—in more ways than one. On the set of *Guinness World Records Unleashed* in 2013, he snapped 19 baseball bats—the **most baseball bats broken with the back in one minute**.

No bottle opener? No problem! Not if Murali K. C. of India is around. He set the record for **most bottle caps removed by the teeth in one minute**, yanking 68 lids off their bottles on September 17, 2011.

Some earrings get pretty heavy, but most folks wouldn't even contemplate swinging something like this from their ears! Johnny Strange isn't most folks, though. He set the record for **heaviest weight lifted by pierced ears** when he heaved a 32-pound, 13.5-ounce weight on October 12, 2013. Those are some strong ears, Johnny!

The **most yardsticks broken with the head in one minute** is 42 and was achieved by Ashrita Furman at the Sri Chinmoy Centre, New York City, on September 18, 2013.

The **heaviest house pulled by a man** weighed 79,145 pounds. The mighty Kevin Fast of Canada pulled this house a distance of 39 feet on September 18, 2010.

Most people blow out candles with their breath, but the **most candles extinguished with a braided pigtail in one minute** is 26! This record was achieved by Anuradha I. Mandal of India, on the set of *Guinness World Records—Ab India Todega* in Mumbai, India, on February 11, 2011.

According to the Sword Swallowers Association International (SSAI), the **youngest male sword-swallower** is Erik Kloeker. Kloeker swallowed a solid steel sword up to the hilt at the age of 16 years, 267 days, on July 21, 2006.

Escapologist Zdeněk Bradáč of the Czech Republic knows how to get himself out of a sticky situation. In fact, on September 9, 2009, he managed to remove multiple handcuffs while at the bottom of a swimming pool to set the record for **fastest time to escape from three pairs of handcuffs underwater**: a lightning-quick 38.69 seconds!

On October 12, 2013, Johnny Strange quickly cut through 10 melons on the body of his stage partner Daniella D'Ville to earn them the title of **most melons chopped on the stomach on a bed of nails in one minute**. The same record without the bed of nails belongs to Ashrita Furman, who had 48 watermelons chopped by Bipin Larkin in a minute.

The **most watermelons crushed with the head in one minute** is 43 and was achieved by Tafzi Ahmed of Germany at the Rose Festival on May 27, 2011.

IT'S A BALANCING ACT!

As you've probably noticed, Daniella D'Ville often takes part in some pretty scary records, along with her partner Johnny Strange, including everything from chain saws to sledgehammers! But she is also a solo daredevil act. On October 12, 2013, she achieved the **most rotations of a sword balanced on a dagger in one minute**: nine!

John Evans of the UK held up a gutted Mini car weighing 352 pounds for 33 seconds on May 24, 1999. That's a record for **heaviest car balanced on the head**!

The **longest duration for a continuous fire blow** is 9.968 seconds! The feat, sometimes known as Dragon's Breath, was achieved by Swedish performer Fredrik Karlsson on November 19, 2011.

CHIN UP!

Ashrita Furman gained another world record on September 15, 2013, when he balanced a chain saw on his chin for 1 minute, 42.47 seconds. This beat his previous time by more than 17 seconds, ensuring that he still held the record for **longest time balancing a chain saw on the chin**.

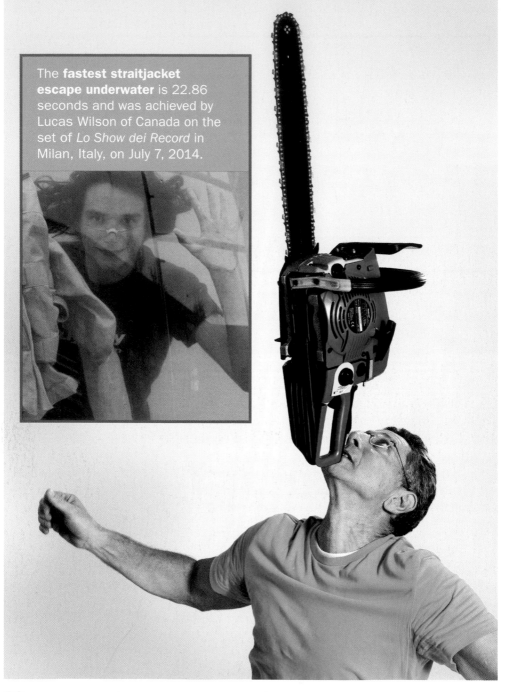

The **fastest straitjacket escape underwater** is 22.86 seconds and was achieved by Lucas Wilson of Canada on the set of *Lo Show dei Record* in Milan, Italy, on July 7, 2014.

You may have noticed some repeat offenders in this book so far—folks who hold more than one Guinness World Records title. Johnny Strange and Daniella D'Ville turn up a lot. So does Chayne Hultgren.

But the guy who has them all beat for sheer number of outrageous and wacky records is Ashrita Furman. He has set, at last count in May 2014, 521 Guinness World Records! Although many of those have been broken since he set them, Furman still holds the Guinness World Records title for **most Guinness World Records titles held**!

Ashrita was born in 1954 in Brooklyn, New York. He changed his name from Keith to Ashrita in 1974. In 1979, he achieved his first Guinness World Records title by doing 27,000 jumping jacks! Since then he has set hundreds more new records. When he isn't eating Smarties blindfolded, playing hopscotch for 24 hours, or catching tennis balls in a bucket on his head, Ashrita manages a health food store in Queens, New York.

Chair race, fastest 100 meters: 38.44 seconds

Farthest champagne cork spitting: 28 feet, 0.61 inches

Farthest distance blowing a Malteser with a straw: 46 feet, 1 inch

Farthest distance carrying a 9-pound brick nonstop (male): 85.05 miles

Farthest distance cycling underwater: 1.87 miles

Farthest distance jumped underwater on pogo stick: 1,680 feet

Farthest distance on unicycle underwater: 1.3 miles

Farthest distance to blow a coin: 16 feet, 2.76 inches

Farthest distance to blow a pea: 22 feet, 2.93 inches

Farthest distance traveled controlling a golf ball: 1.8 miles

Farthest distance traveled controlling a golf ball between two clubs: 1,382 feet, 8.88 inches

Farthest distance walked balancing a baseball bat on finger: 9 miles

Farthest distance walked balancing a lawn mower on the chin (not powered): 328 feet, 2.88 inches

Farthest distance walked balancing a lawn mower on the chin (powered): 65 feet, 62 inches

Farthest water balloon throw: 127 feet, 4.32 inches

Fastest one-mile run wearing swim fins (individual, male): 7 minutes, 47.25 seconds

Fastest 10 meters balancing pool cue on chin: 3.02 seconds

Fastest 10 meters frog jumping: 8.22 seconds

Fastest 100 meters carrying an egg on a spoon in the mouth: 21.94 seconds

Fastest 100 meters frog jumping: 7 minutes, 18 seconds

Fastest 100 meters on a space hopper (male): 30.2 seconds

Fastest 400 meters on spring-loaded stilts: 1 minute, 32.78 seconds

Fastest 5 kilometers joggling in swim fins: 32 minutes, 3 seconds

Fastest 5 kilometers skipping without a rope: 30 minutes

Fastest game of hopscotch: 1 minute, 1.97 seconds

Fastest half marathon balancing a milk bottle on the head: 2 hours, 33 minutes, 28 seconds

Fastest half marathon skipping without a rope: 2 hours, 27 minutes, 1 second

Fastest marathon skipping without a rope: 5 hours, 55 minutes, 13 seconds

Fastest mile balancing a baseball bat on a finger: 7 minutes, 5 seconds

Fastest mile balancing a book on head: 8 minutes, 27 seconds

Fastest mile bounce juggling three objects (male): 7 minutes, 27 seconds

Fastest mile carrying an egg on a spoon in the mouth: 9 minutes, 29 seconds

Fastest mile Hula-Hooping (male): 11 minutes, 21.06 seconds

Fastest mile Hula-Hooping while balancing a milk bottle on the head: 13 minutes, 37.35 seconds

Fastest mile in a fireman's uniform: 7 minutes, 58.02 seconds

Fastest mile jumping on a pogo ball: 43 minutes, 9 seconds

Fastest mile on a pogo stick while dribbling a basketball: 23 minutes, 2.9 seconds

Fastest mile on a space hopper: 13 minutes

Fastest mile on pogo stick while juggling three balls: 23 minutes, 28 seconds

Fastest mile on spring-loaded stilts: 7 minutes, 13 seconds

Fastest mile skipping with a rope while wearing swim fins: 14 minutes, 14.65 seconds

Fastest mile spinning a whip top: 25 minutes, 13 seconds

Fastest mile traveled balancing a pool cue on finger: 6 minutes, 55 seconds

Fastest mile walking on shovels: 24 minutes, 0.25 seconds

Fastest sack race one mile: 16 minutes, 41 seconds

Fastest stilt-walker 8 kilometers: 39 minutes, 56 seconds

Fastest stilt-walker one mile: 12 minutes, 23 seconds

Fastest string can stilt-walking one mile: 11 minutes, 55 seconds

Fastest time to balance a dozen eggs: 1 minute, 15.72 seconds

Fastest time to cross 10 meters on lightbulbs: 6.89 seconds

Fastest time to drink 200 milliliters of mustard: 20.80 seconds

Fastest time to dry-bob six marshmallows: 27.50 seconds

Fastest time to duct-tape a person to a wall: 32.85 seconds

Fastest time to duct-tape yourself to a wall: 2 minutes, 12.63 seconds

Fastest time to Hula-Hoop 10 kilometers (male): 1 hour, 25 minutes, 9 seconds

Fastest time to peel and eat a kiwi fruit: 5.35 seconds

Fastest time to peel and eat a lemon: 8.25 seconds

Fastest time to peel and eat three kiwi fruits: 21.1 seconds

Fastest time to peel and eat three oranges: 1 minute, 9.72 seconds

Fastest time to pogo-stick-jump up the CN Tower: 57 minutes, 51 seconds

Fastest time to run a mile while balancing a milk bottle on the head: 7 minutes, 47 seconds

Fastest time to walk 10 meters backward in iron shoes: 32.97 seconds

Forward rolls, one mile (gym): 19 minutes, 11 seconds

Giant Hula-Hoop—most rotations in one minute: 64 (record shared with Georgos "Spilly" Spiliadis)

Golf ball control, one club—duration: 1 hour, 20 minutes, 42 seconds

Greatest distance juggling on a pogo stick: 4 miles, 30 feet

Greatest distance to spit a table tennis ball: 42 feet, 1.2 inches

Greatest distance traveled with a pool cue balanced on chin: 5,472 feet, 9 inches

Greatest distance traveled with pool cue balanced on a finger: 8.95 miles

Greatest distance walked balancing a book on head: 20 miles

Greatest distance walked with a milk bottle balanced on the head: 80.96 miles

Heaviest milk-crate stack balanced on chin: 93 pounds, 7 ounces

Heaviest shoes walked in: 323 pounds

Heaviest weight transferred hand to hand 100 times: 44.09 pounds

Highest mountain climbed on stilts: 9,398 feet, 11 inches

Highest vertical height walked on stilts: 4,018 feet

Largest Hula-Hoop spun: 16 feet, 6.7 inches

Largest incense stick: 31 feet, 7.53 inches (length)

Largest pencil: 76 feet, 2.75 inches (length)

Largest tennis racket: 50 feet, 3.07 inches (length)

Longest duration balancing a chain saw on a chin: 1 minute, 42.47 seconds

Longest duration balancing a ladder on the chin: 4 minutes, 9.22 seconds

Longest duration balancing a lawn mower on the chin (not powered): 5 minutes, 1 second

Longest duration balancing a lawn mower on the chin (powered): 3 minutes, 1.34 seconds

Longest duration balancing a pool cue on one finger: 4 hours, 7 minutes

Longest duration balancing an object on the nose: 31 minutes, 0.01 second

Longest egg-table-tennis rally: 14 touches

Longest seesaw/teeter-totter: 79 feet, 2 inches

Longest time standing on a globe: 43 minutes, 56 seconds

Longest time to Hula-Hoop underwater: 2 minutes, 38 seconds

Longest time to pogo-stick-jump underwater: 3 hours, 40 minutes

Longest time to stand on a Swiss ball: 5 hours, 7 minutes, 6 seconds

Most apples cut in the air by sword in one minute: 29

Most apples sliced on a pogo stick in one minute: 39 (record shared with Bipin Larkin)

Most apples snapped in one minute: 44

Most baked beans eaten in three minutes: 152

Most balloons blown up in one hour (individual): 671

Most balloons burst by sitting in 30 seconds: 37

Most balloons burst by sitting in one minute: 58

Most balloons burst using a fork in one minute: 197

Most balloons inflated by the nose in one hour: 380

Most balloons inflated by the nose in three minutes: 28

Most bananas sliced with a sword on a slack line in one minute: 36

Most bananas snapped in one minute: 99

Most baseballs held in a baseball glove: 26

Most basketball neck catches in one minute: 27

Most beer mats flipped and caught in 30 seconds: 40

Most beer mats flipped and caught in one minute: 74

Most blowtorches extinguished with the tongue in one minute: 31

Most boiled eggs peeled and eaten in one minute: 6

Most boiled eggs thrown and caught in the mouth in one minute: 50

Most candles on a cake: 48,523

Most CDs balanced on one finger: 50

Most CDs flipped and caught in one minute: 80

Most champagne bottles sabered in one minute: 40

Most champagne corks popped in one minute: 10

Most chopsticks broken with the fist in one minute: 106

Most chopsticks snapped in 30 seconds: 60

Most chopsticks snapped in one minute: 118

Most chopsticks thrown at a target in one minute: 14

Most Christmas crackers pulled in one minute by a team of two: 52 (shared with Bipin Larkin)

Most cigar boxes balanced on chin: 223

Most consecutive forward rolls: 8,341

Most consecutive passes of a giant inflatable ball: 1,300 (shared with Bipin Larkin)

Most cucumbers chopped blindfolded on the hand in one minute: 65 (shared with Homagni Baptista)

Most cucumbers sliced from a person's mouth with a sword in one minute: 27

Most cucumbers snapped in one minute: 118

Most darts caught by hand in one minute: 20 (shared with Bipin Larkin)

Most drink cans crushed by hand while holding an egg in 30 seconds: 23

Most drinks with a ring pull opened in 30 seconds: 41

Most drinks with a ring pull opened in one minute: 66

Most eggs balanced by an individual: 888

Most eggs crushed with the toes in 30 seconds: 39

Most eggs crushed with the toes in one minute: 55

Most eggs thrown and caught in one minute (team of two): 87 (shared with Bipin Larkin)

Most eggs thrown and then caught with the mouth in one minute: 12 (shared with Bipin Larkin)

Most forward rolls in one hour (individual): 1,330

Most games of hopscotch played in one hour: 33

Most garland exchanges by a team of two in one minute: 37 (shared with Bipin Larkin)

Most grapes caught by mouth in one minute: 86

Most grapes eaten in three minutes: 190

Most hagoita hits between two people in one minute: 89 (shared with Bipin Larkin)

Most hits of a person with water balloons in one minute: 32 (shared with Bipin Larkin)

Most hopscotch games in 24 hours: 434

Most ice-cream scoops balanced on a cone: 100

Most jelly eaten with chopsticks in one minute: 1 pound, 5 ounces

Most knives caught in one minute: 54 (shared with Bipin Larkin)

Most lemons caught blindfolded in 30 seconds (team of two): 15 (shared with Bipin Larkin)

Most lemons caught blindfolded in one minute (team of two): 29 (shared with Bipin Larkin)

Most Maltesers thrown and then caught with the mouth in one minute: 76 (shared with Bipin Larkin)

Most Marmite eaten in one minute: 7.6 ounces

Most marshmallows caught with chopsticks in one minute: 31 (shared with Bipin Larkin)

Most marshmallows dry-bobbed in one minute: 20

Most mashed potatoes eaten in one minute: 1 pound, 11.2 ounces

Most mustard (tube) drunk in 30 seconds: 13.55 ounces

Most olives eaten in one minute: 60

Most oranges peeled and eaten in three minutes: 6

Most pancakes thrown and caught in one minute (team of two): 46 (shared with Bipin Larkin)

Most paper aircrafts caught by mouth in one minute: 17 (shared with Bipin Larkin)

Most party-poppers popped in 30 seconds: 38

Most party-poppers popped in one minute: 64

Most Ping-Pong balls caught with chopsticks in one minute: 32

Most pint glasses balanced on the chin: 81

Most pogo-stick peg taps in 30 seconds: 62

Most popping popcorn caught with both hands in one minute: 34

Most potatoes cut by jumping on a shovel in one minute: 38

Most shaving-cream pies thrown in one minute by a team of two: 71 (shared with Bipin Larkin)

Most single garland passes in one minute: 77 (shared with Bipin Larkin)

Most skips of a rope wearing clogs in one minute: 127

Most skips of a rope wearing swim fins in one minute: 113

Most skips on a pogo stick in one minute (male): 178

Most skips on spring-loaded stilts in one minute: 145

Most Smarties eaten in one minute blindfolded using chopsticks: 20

Most spears caught from a speargun above water in one minute: 13

Most spoons twisted in one minute: 14

Most stairs climbed while balancing books on the head in one minute: 122

Most surgical gloves inflated in two minutes: 4

Most tennis balls caught in a basket on the back in one minute: 66 (shared with Bipin Larkin)

Most T-shirts torn in one minute: 24

Most T-shirts worn and torn in one minute: 25

Most underwater rope-jumps in one hour: 900

Most underwater rope-jumps in one hour (scuba): 1,608

Most vinyl records smashed in 30 seconds (individual): 38

Most walnuts crushed by the hand in one minute: 131

Most watermelons chopped on the stomach in one minute: 48 (shared with Bipin Larkin)

Most wet sponges thrown in one minute (two people): 43 (shared with Bipin Larkin)

Orange nose-push—fastest mile: 22 minutes, 41 seconds

Pogo-stick jumping—fastest mile: 12 minutes, 16 seconds

Sack race—fastest 10 kilometers: 1 hour, 22 minutes, 2 seconds

Shortest usable pogo stick: 18.16 inches

Space hopper—greatest distance in 24 hours: 5 miles

Spinning top—duration: 7 hours, 1 minute, 14 seconds

Tallest object balanced on chin: 68 feet, 11.36 inches

Tiddlywinks—farthest distance traveled in 24 hours: 4.04 miles (shared with Bipin Larkin)

Tiddlywinks—fastest mile (individual): 23 minutes, 22 seconds

Tinned-pea-eating—three minutes: 222

SECTION SIX:

AMAZING BODY

Can your tongue do this? Most of us have some little trick we can do with our body. . . . Maybe you can bend your thumb backward or touch your tongue to your nose. Maybe you can wiggle your ears!

But the people who have set Guinness World Records with their amazing bodies are in a whole other league. Read on to witness some of the wildest acts of strength, flexibility, and bravery you've ever dreamed of!

The **most balloons inflated by the nose in one hour** is 380, achieved by Ashrita Furman, at the Sri Chinmoy Centre in Queens, New York, on March 3, 2013.

The **most fingers and toes** on a living person is 28—14 fingers and 14 toes—which belong to Devendra Suthar from India, as verified in Himatnagar, Gujarat, India, on November 11, 2014. Devendra's extra digits are caused by a condition known as polydactylism.

I'VE GOT A CRUSH ON YOU . . .

Linsey Lindberg shows no mercy when it comes to apples. Lindberg set the record for **most apples crushed with the bicep in one minute** by smashing 10 apples on the set of *Lo Show dei Record* in Milan, Italy, on July 3, 2014, beating her own record by two apples.

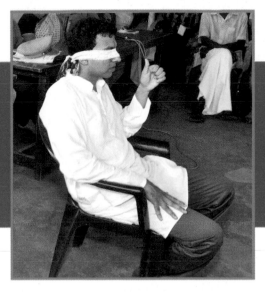

Like the mythical wizard Merlin, Preijesh Merlin of Kannur, India, performed a trick that seems like it must be magic! Setting a record for the **most random objects memorized**, Merlin recalled 470 random items in the order they were read to him on June 23, 2012.

A good memory is a wonderful thing! And Canadian Dave Farrow's memory is better than good! After seeing them only once, Farrow memorized the order of 59 separate packs of cards, setting the record for the **most decks of playing cards memorized in a single sighting**. The attempt took 4 hours, 58 minutes, 20 seconds, not including breaks.

MIND-BENDING!

Super-bendy Leilani Franco from the Philippines and the UK is the world record holder for **most full-body revolutions maintaining a chest stand**, completing 29 in the 60-second time limit, on July 21, 2014.

FACT!

A chest stand is a position in which a person rests their body on the floor (facedown) and their legs bend over the head so that the feet rest on the floor in front of the face/head. In order to count as a full revolution, both legs must complete a 360-degree revolution around the body before returning to the original starting position.

Shristi Dharmendra Sharma of India was 10 years old when she achieved the **lowest limbo skating over 10 meters** (32 feet, 9.6 inches). Sharma limboed to a ground-scraping 6.5 inches in Nagpur, Maharashtra, India, on August 23, 2014.

Medvin Deva, also from India, went to even greater lengths to earn his record. He achieved the **lowest limbo skating over 25 meters** (82 feet), reaching as low as 9 inches off the ground at the Jawaharlal Nehru Indoor Stadium skating ring in Chennai, Tamil Nadu, India, on February 22, 2014.

The **longest fingernails ever for a woman** belonged to Lee Redmond. She started to grow them in 1979 and carefully tended them until they reached a total length of 28 feet, 4.5 inches. This record-setting length was officially measured on February 23, 2008.

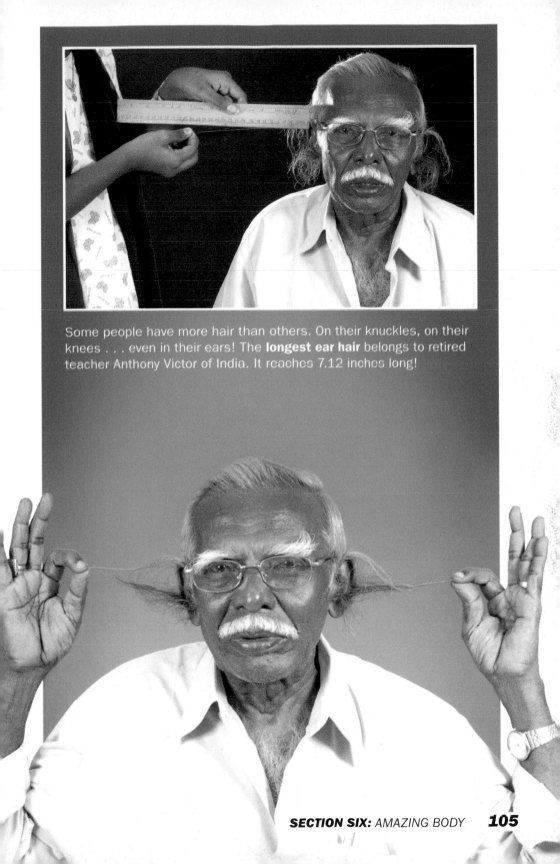

Some people have more hair than others. On their knuckles, on their knees . . . even in their ears! The **longest ear hair** belongs to retired teacher Anthony Victor of India. It reaches 7.12 inches long!

The **longest hair for a female** is 18 feet, 6 inches long! This amazing head of hair belongs to Xie Qiuping of China, and was measured on May 8, 2004. How long would it take you to grow your hair that long? Xie Qiuping stopped cutting her hair in 1973 . . . when she was 13!

THE HEIGHTS OF FASHION!

The world's **highest hairstyle** is 8.73-plus feet tall and was created by several hairdressers on June 21, 2009. It was taller than just about every human being who ever lived! (Except, of course, the Guinness World Records holder of **tallest man ever**, who stood 8 feet, 11.1 inches tall.) The hairstyle was made with a mix of real and fake hair.

How much can one measly haircut possibly cost? A *lot*, it turns out! The **most expensive haircut** cost $16,420 on October 29, 2009. The barber was Stuart Phillips at the Stuart Phillips Salon in Covent Garden, London, UK. The record-breaking haircut package included a champagne lunch, a head and scalp massage, a selection of personalized hair products and treatments, a return limousine ride from the airport, and of course, the haircutting skills of Stuart Phillips himself. Beverley Lateo of Pisa, Italy, was the happy customer.

The **fastest haircut** is 49.76 seconds and was achieved by Roberto A. Gangale at Carlo's Barbershop, in Broadview Heights, Ohio, on November 18, 2011. The speedy cut beat the previous record by more than five seconds and was performed on the mayor of Broadview Heights.

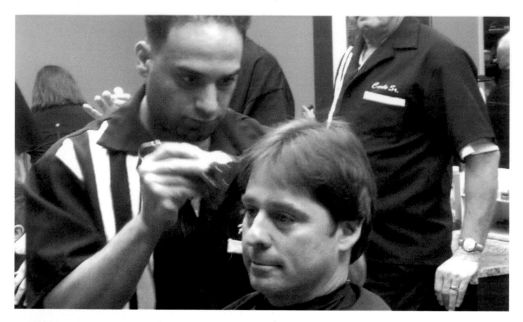

Sarwan Singh of Canada has a beard that's taller than he is! It's the **longest beard on a living man**, and it measures 8 feet, 2.5 inches. The first time Singh's beard was measured it was 7 feet, 9 inches. Then, two years later in 2011, it was measured again and had grown nearly 6 inches!

The Marinelli bend position is a difficult feat, even for professional contortionists! Holding it for very long is really, really hard. But that didn't stop Iona Luvsandorj of Mongolia from setting the record for **longest time to hold the Marinelli bend position**. She held it for 50 seconds.

And it didn't stop Tsatsral Erdenebileg of Mongolia from breaking that record, on July 17, 2013! Erdenebileg held the Marinelli position for 4 minutes, 17 seconds.

LICKETY SPLIT!

The **most electric fan blades stopped with the tongue** is 32 and was achieved by Zoe Ellis, aka L'Amore, of Australia on July 11, 2014. Zoe used two fans—one in each hand—both of which were set at the highest speed. This record has subsequently been claimed by Ashrita Furman, who stopped 35 fans in one minute on August 14, 2014.

Here's a record not everybody would want to achieve: the **most clothespins clipped to the face in one minute**! The winner of this painful contest is Silvio Sabba of Italy, who on December 27, 2012, clipped 51 clothespins to his face!

SECTION SEVEN

GOOD SPORTS

Welcome to the Oddball Olympics! What's your favorite sport? Whether you're into skateboarding, archery, basketball, or even diving, someone has found a way to turn it into a crazy world record! You won't believe what some of these astonishing athletes are capable of. . . .

The **most balls juggled** is 11. This record was set by Alex Barron of the UK, who managed 23 consecutive catches in what is known as a "qualifying" juggling run, on April 3, 2012.

Alex Barron was 18 years old at the time of the attempt. He had spent two years practicing for this moment. The juggling record had not been broken for 16 years. On the day in question, he spent four and a half hours in a squash court trying to reach his target. He was getting pretty tired by the time he finally achieved this number!

Barron also jointly holds the record for **most balls flashed by a juggler**. In 2012, Barron also flash-juggled the most beanbags: 13. Flashing is different from a qualifying run as it only requires each ball to be thrown and caught once.

Sure, lots of people like to skateboard. But how many skateboarders have gone faster than the highway speed limit? Meet Mischo Erban of Canada, who set the world record on June 18, 2012. Erban's record for **fastest skateboard speed, standing** is 80.74 miles per hour!

The **longest time holding a person overhead vertically** is 1 minute, 16 seconds. This amazing feat of strength was achieved by Markus Ferber and Clarissa Beyelschmidt (both from Germany) on March 11, 2010.

Ah, there's nothing like a clean dive off a tall diving board into . . . a foot of water? That's a pretty risky dive! The **highest shallow dive** was from a height of 37 feet, 11 inches into 12 inches of water and was achieved by Darren Taylor (aka Professor Splash) on the set of *CCTV—Guinness World Records Special* in Xiamen, Fujian, China, on September 9, 2014.

Some people would be pretty proud to set a record for running a marathon, but Elizabeth King of the UK wanted to go one further. With her finishing time of 4 hours, 13 minutes, 24 seconds, King ran the **fastest marathon dressed as a fruit by a female**. She completed the race in a strawberry costume.

ONE HOT BIKE RIDE!

The **fastest crossing of the Sahara Desert by bicycle** took 13 days, 5 hours, 50 minutes, 14 seconds, set by Reza Pakravan of Iran in 2011. The sweltering bike race started in Algeria and concluded in Sudan. The total distance cycled was 1,083.85 miles.

The **longest duration juggling three objects while suspended upside down** is 12 minutes, 50 seconds. Professional juggler and circus performer Quinn Spicker from Canada set this record on July 22, 2010, in Vancouver, British Columbia.

The **longest duration spinning a basketball on the head** was 18.11 seconds by Mehmet Kekec of Germany at the Soccer Meets Schanze charity event in Hamburg, on May 28, 2011. Kekec began by spinning the ball on his finger, before moving it to his head when the official attempt began.

Running in armor probably makes a lot of noise. When Peter Pedersen of Denmark set the record for **fastest marathon wearing armor**, he was making noise for 6 hours, 46 minutes, 59 seconds. Peter clinked, clanked, and clonked his way into the record books on September 21, 2008. He wore full medieval battle armor—including boots, helmet, and gauntlets. The total weight was 62 pounds!

ROPE 'EM, COWBOY!

The record for the **largest trick roping loop by a male** was achieved by Charlie Keyes. He spun a loop around himself using 107 feet, 2 inches of rope at the Will Rogers International Wild West Expo in Claremore, Oklahoma, on April 22, 2006.

On June 4, 2006, sharpshooter Luis Caídas Martín of Spain set the **fastest time to shoot 10 arrows**—1 minute, 7 seconds.

The **fastest football kick by a machine** is 139.8 miles per hour. This remarkable robotic kicker was built by Castrol Ichi-Go in Japan. The record-setting soccer kick (football is the British term, of course!) took place at Olympic Plaza of National Yoyogi Stadium, Tokyo, Japan, on June 19, 2010.

How nimble are your toes? Can you pick things up with them? Wiggle them separately? Here are some truly fantastic feet: they fired an arrow into a target from 20 feet away—the **farthest arrow shot using feet**. Nancy Siefker achieved this feat on the set of *Guinness World Records Unleashed* in Los Angeles, California, on June 20, 2013.

Running five kilometers (3.1 miles) is no joke. Running five kilometers while juggling three balls is also no joke. Running five kilometers in swimming fins while juggling three balls . . . well, that's pretty funny. But it's also really hard! Ashrita Furman set the record for **fastest five kilometers joggling in swim fins** when he managed it in 32 minutes, 3 seconds. This astonishing record was set on May 30, 2012, in Houštka, Czech Republic.

The **fastest marathon dressed as a snowman** is 3 hours, 47 minutes, 39 seconds. Congratulations to David Smith of the UK, who set this record at the Luton Marathon in Luton, Bedfordshire, UK, on November 20, 2011!

Climbing a pole is hard enough, but doing it while you're upside down is nearly impossible! In 60 seconds, the remarkable Nele Bruckmann of Germany managed to ascend 31 feet, 11 inches feet first! She set the **farthest distance climbed up a pole upside down in one minute** on the set of *Guinness World Records—Die größten Weltrekorde* in Cologne, Germany, on September 1, 2007.

FROSTY THE TOE-MAN!

If Wim Hof of the Netherlands didn't get cold feet before taking on this record, he certainly must have during the attempt! He ran the **fastest half marathon while barefoot on ice/snow** in 2 hours, 16 minutes, 34 seconds, near Oulu, Finland, in 2007.

Joanne Singleton of the UK managed a half marathon—that's 13.1 miles!—in just 1 hour, 35 minutes, 45 seconds. And here's the best part . . . she was dressed as a strawberry while she did it! That makes Singleton the female holder of the Guinness World Records title for **fastest half marathon dressed as a fruit**.

JUST WING IT!

The **oldest wing-walker** is Thomas Lackey of the UK. At the age of 93 years, 100 days, he completed a wing walk between Stranraer, Scotland, and Derry, Northern Ireland, on August 29, 2013. Lackey has held this record four times in the past and completed his first wing walk when he was in his 80s.

FACT!
Wing-walking is when a passenger stands on or moves around the wing of a plane while it is in flight.

The **longest wingsuit flight** is 9 minutes, 6 seconds, and was achieved by Jhonathan Florez above La Guajira, Colombia, on April 20, 2012.

The **fastest marathon dressed as a Mr. Potato Head** was run in 3 hours, 38 minutes, 20 seconds. The potato in question was Andrew McKenzie of Australia, who ran his record-setting race on October 14, 2012.

Rimas Kinka of Lithuania holds the world record for the **longest distance kite surfing in 24 hours**. Kinka made it 401.2 miles off the coast of Islamorada, Florida, on February 26, 2012.

The **fastest one-mile sack race** was completed in 16 minutes, 41 seconds by Ashrita Furman in Baruun Salaa in Mongolia, on May 19, 2007. Cheering him on throughout the attempt was a local man and his yak!

Juggling three balls while hanging upside down is hard enough, but add a fourth ball and you're in Guinness World Records territory! Zdeněk Bradáč of the Czech Republic juggled four balls while suspended with gravity boots on November 1, 2010, earning him the title for the **most balls juggled while suspended upside down**!

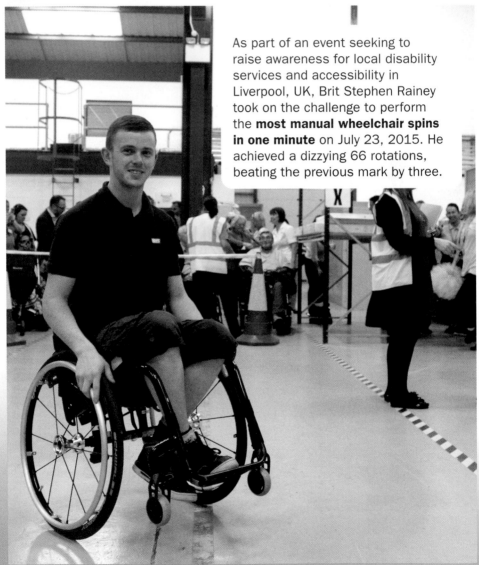

As part of an event seeking to raise awareness for local disability services and accessibility in Liverpool, UK, Brit Stephen Rainey took on the challenge to perform the **most manual wheelchair spins in one minute** on July 23, 2015. He achieved a dizzying 66 rotations, beating the previous mark by three.

Marawa Ibrahim of Australia knows how to get some real speed in skates . . . even when those skates are high-heeled! Marawa the Amazing, as she is also known, set the record for **fastest 100 meters (328 feet) on high-heeled roller skates** on August 21, 2013. She covered the distance in just 26.1 seconds!

The **most artistic cycling rounds in a row while holding the raiser head tube reverse shoulder-stand position** is four. This remarkable record was set by super-talented sisters Carla and Henriette Hochdorfer from Germany on the set of *Lo Show dei Record* in Rome, Italy, on March 18, 2010.

The **most bowling balls juggled** is three! This heavy record was set by Milan Roskopf of Slovakia. Each ball weighed 10 pounds, and Roskopf juggled them for 28.69 seconds at the Prague juggling marathon, in the Czech Republic, on November 19, 2011.

SECTIO
EIGHT:
TOTALLY
RANDOM

Let's get random! There are lots of things you can do to earn a Guinness World Records title. . . . You can be great at sports or have the biggest collection of something. You can build a wacky car or you can have the heaviest bunny rabbit. There are all sorts of categories of records you can enter.

But some records just can't be put in any category because they are too unique . . . too random! The last section of this book is filled with nothing but the most bizarre, unconventional, and baffling records there are!

N

Did you know it's possible to roll a frying pan into a frying-pan burrito? You have to be *incredibly* strong. The record for **most frying pans rolled in one minute by a male** is held by Steven Weiner. On January 10, 2015, at the Venetian Theatre in Macau, China, he rolled 14 frying pans in a minute.

"Gurning" means making faces. Did you know there are gurning contests, to see who can make the ugliest face? There's even a Gurning World Championship! The record for **winning the most Gurning World Championships by a male** belongs to Tommy Mattinson of the UK, whose flexible face took the top prize 14 times!

The **tallest swing** is in South Africa, and was constructed on May 14, 2011, by B!g Rush. It's 288 feet, 8 inches from the seat of the swing to the crossbar it hangs from!

136

To celebrate the 75th convention of the US National Federation of the Blind (NFB), the organization arranged a rather unusual record attempt using umbrellas—and in the Sunshine State of all places! A total of 2,480 participants achieved the **largest umbrella mosaic** on July 8, 2015, re-creating the NFB's logo and spelling out the words "Live the Life You Want," all with umbrellas.

Henna tattoos are made by drawing designs on the skin using henna paste. When the paste dries and flakes off, it leaves a stain on the skin. These tattoos aren't permanent, but they can last for a while! Henna tattoos are usually very complicated, so it takes a while to create them. Pavan Ahluwalia of the UK is so fast, though, that she set the record for the **most henna tattoos completed in one hour**: 511! This world record was set on February 27, 2012.

The record was set at Goodmayes Primary School in Ilford, UK. A total of 256 participants took part in the event. Each individual received two henna armband tattoos, one on each arm.

The world's **largest shoe** is 20 feet, 11.97 inches by 7 feet, 10.09 inches and it stands 5 foot, 4.96 inches tall. It was created by Electric Sekki in Hong Kong, China, on April 12, 2013.

When people get dental caps, they're usually very small—a fraction of the size of a human tooth. But the world's **largest dental caps** don't belong to a person. They belong to an Asian elephant. Spike's tusk caps are 19 inches long and 5 inches in diameter. They weigh 28 pounds each. Spike's caps were attached to his cracked tusks in a 3-hour, 30-minute operation on July 4, 2002, in Alberta, Canada. The caps are made of stainless steel.

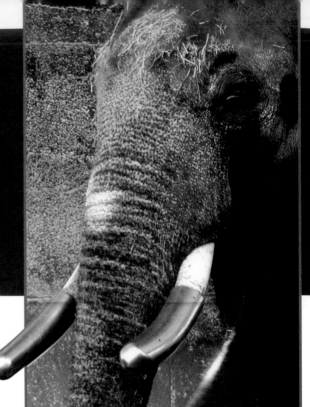

BELLY-BUSTING!
The **longest belly-dance shimmy** is 3 hours, 7 seconds. This wriggly record was set by Melanie White of Australia on February 25, 2012.

Suresh Joachim of Sri Lanka holds the Guinness World Records title for **longest time to balance on one foot**. He stood on one foot for 76 hours, 40 minutes! This astonishing feat of endurance took place from May 22 to 25, 1997.

The **longest frog jump** covered 3 feet, 11.64 inches. This lengthy leap was made by Noa Möller of Sweden on November 19, 2011.

I SCREAM, YOU SCREAM, BUT SHE SCREAMS THE LOUDEST SCREAM!

Classroom assistant Jill Drake of the UK produced the **loudest scream by an individual** on Halloween day in 2000, at the Millennium Dome in London. Her scream reached 129 dB!

The **largest Russian nesting doll** is a 51-piece set hand-painted by Youlia Bereznitskaia of Russia. The largest doll in Bereznitskaia's record-smashing set measures 1 foot, 9.25 inches high, while the smallest is 0.125 inches. The set was completed on April 25, 2003. When all 51 pieces in this set of nesting dolls are lined up together touching, they measure 11 feet, 2.25 inches long.

The **tallest toilet-roll pyramid** is 13 feet, 5 inches high! It was built by Ivan Zarif Neto, Rafael Migani Monteiro, and Fernando Gama (all from Brazil), in São Paulo, Brazil, on November 20, 2012. The structure was made of 23,821 separate rolls!

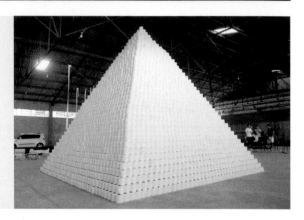

Just imagine what kind of monster crayon you'd need to fill in the **largest coloring book**. . . . The supersize coloring book measured 107.63 square feet and was created by Polish children's publisher Wydawnictwo Zielona Sowa (Green Owl Publishing House), as verified at the National Stadium in Warsaw, Poland, on May 24, 2014.

I SEE LONDON . . . I SEE FRANCE . . .

You can probably see these underpants from a mile away! The **largest underpants** are 65 feet, 7 inches across the waist, and 39 feet, 4 inches from waistband to crotch. They were presented by Pants to Poverty in London, UK, on September 16, 2010.

It must have sounded like Yahoo!'s headquarters in Sunnyvale, California, had been transported to the Swiss Alps on November 19, 2004. That was the day that 1,795 people came together to achieve the **largest simultaneous yodel**. After months of planning, the singing part of the Yahoo! Yodel Challenge lasted for just over a minute.

The **largest published book** is an edition of *The Little Prince,* which was published by Eidouro Gráfica e Editora, Ltda. of Brazil, on September 13, 2007. This voluminous volume—which is anything but little in any way, shape, or form—is 6 feet, 7 inches tall and 10 feet, 1 inch wide when open. It has 128 pages.

James Peters of the UK became the record holder for **most straitjacket escapes in eight hours** on September 27, 2003! He set himself free a staggering 193 times in the allocated time. He completed his fastest escape in just 56 seconds!

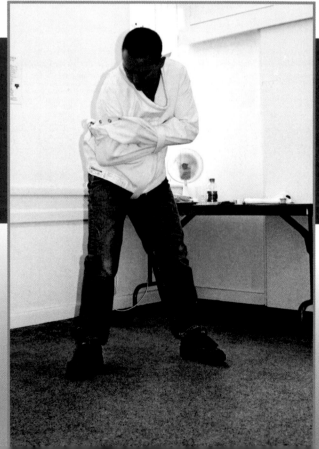

Shishir Hathwar of India holds the record for the **fastest backward spelling of 50 words**! He achieved this in 1 minute, 22.53 seconds. This *gnizama* record was set on November 13, 2010!

The record for **people crammed in a photo booth** is seven! This record was set by Photo-Me International in King's Cross train station, London, UK, on July 4, 2012.

DO YOU WANNA BUILD A SNOWMAN?

How about 2,036 of them? That's how many Drama 24 Unhandy Handyman of Japan built on February 28, 2015, at Zuriyama Observation Field, in Hokkaido, Japan, to achieve the record of **most snowmen built in one hour**.

This record requires some flexibility! Skye Broberg of New Zealand became the record holder for **fastest time to cram into a box** when she managed to squeeze herself into one in just 4.78 seconds! Broberg set this record on September 15, 2011. The box she climbed into was a tiny 20.5 by 17.7 by 17.7 inches. Once Broberg's body was entirely inside the box, the lid was closed from the outside. The clock was stopped once the lid was closed.

Being a champion is one thing, but it's even cooler to be the champion of winning championships! Zac "The Magnet" Monro from the UK (pictured) and Ochi "Dianoji" Yosuke from Japan both hold the record for **most wins in the Air Guitar World Championship**. They have each won two championships to date. Monro was victorious in 2001 and 2002, and Yosuke won the titles in 2006 and 2007!

TEXTING AT THE SPEED OF LOL!

Think you're a speedy texter? Wait until you hear about Elliot Nicholls of New Zealand. He achieved the **fastest time to send a text message while blindfolded** on November 17, 2007—45.09 seconds! The GWR-approved message he typed was "The razor-toothed piranhas of the genera *Serrasalmus* and *Pygocentrus* are the most ferocious freshwater fish in the world. In reality they seldom attack a human."

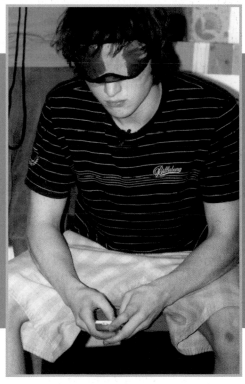

Everyone loves party balloons, and we bet you've wondered how many helium-filled balloons you'd need to fly, right? Well, Mike Howard and Steve Davies found out that they needed 1,400 of them on August 4, 2001, in order to set the world record for **highest altitude reached by helium balloons**: 18,300 feet!

The **most clothespins clipped on the face at once** is 161! This painful and impressive record was set by Garry Turner of the UK in Istanbul, Turkey, on July 17, 2013.

YOU KNOW, THERE'S THIS THING CALLED THE SNOOZE BUTTON. . . .

Why use the snooze button when you can just smash the alarm clock altogether? The record for **most alarm clocks smashed using the feet in one minute** is 88 and was achieved by Jay Wheddon of the UK on October 3, 2008.

The **heaviest shoes walked in** weighed 323 pounds! These boots were used by Ashrita Furman at Potters Fields, London, UK, on Guinness World Records Day, held on November 18, 2010.

On November 15, 2012, Australian Steve Jacobs became the record holder for **most underpants worn at once**. Jacobs managed to get 266 pairs of undies on!

Serial record-breaker Silvio Sabba of Italy doesn't waste any time getting dressed. He earned the record for **most socks put on one foot in one minute**, slipping on 45 socks on May 2, 2013.

The **most people in a decorated hat competition** is 1,343 at an event organized by AMUTER/Municipio de Vila Verde. They donned their festive hats on October 16, 2015, in Braga, Portugal.

The students of Tsugeno High School in Japan worked together to set a world record! All 229 of them helped create this 436-square-foot mosaic made entirely of toothpicks. The **largest toothpick mosaic** was completed on October 5, 2008. It comprised 1,620,840 toothpicks in seven different colors!

DON'T BURST MY BALLOON!

The **fastest time to pop three balloons with the back** is 12 seconds! This back-breaking record was set by Julia Gunthel, aka Zlata, of Germany, on November 23, 2007.

150

The **largest kite flown** has a total lifting area of 10,225.7 square feet. When laid flat, it has a total area of 10,968.4 square feet. The kite is 83 feet, 7 inches long and 131 feet, 3 inches wide. The kite was made by Abdulrahman Al Farsi and Faris Al Farsi, and flown at the Kuwait Hala Festival in, appropriately, Flag Square, Kuwait City, Kuwait, on February 15, 2005.

Ten thousand is the **most balls released**! This record was set on June 5, 2010, in Lisbon, Portugal, at an event to celebrate the start of the 2010 FIFA World Cup.

The **fastest time to ignite five targets by squirting milk from the eye** is 34.9 seconds! Brandon "Youngblood" Kee set this eye-watering record on June 13, 2013.

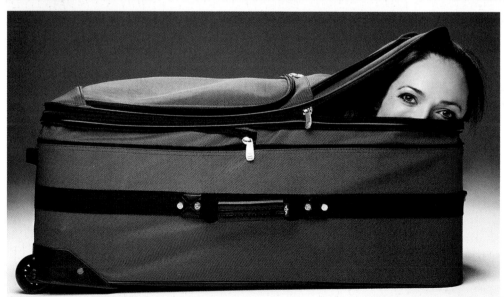

Leslie Tipton holds the record for **fastest time to enter a suitcase**. She managed it in 5.43 seconds on September 14, 2009, on the set of *Live with Regis and Kelly*.

Serial record-breaker Suresh Joachim rocked on a rocking chair continuously for 75 hours, 3 minutes, taking the title for **longest marathon rocking on a rocking chair**. He rocked from August 24 to 27, 2005, at the Hilton Garden Inn, Mississauga, Ontario, Canada.

The **shortest stand-up comedian** is Imaan Hadchiti of Lebanon/Australia, who stands at 3 feet, 4.3 inches tall. He has been doing stand-up in Australia and the UK since 2005.

The **thickest book published** is 12.67 inches thick and was unveiled by HarperCollins in London, UK, on May 20, 2009. The volume is a collection of all of Agatha Christie's Miss Marple stories—12 novels and 20 short stories.

THE BIGGEST BOBBLE!

Standing 11 feet tall and in the likeness of game show host Chuck Woolery, the **largest bobblehead** weighs 900 pounds! It was created by the Game Show Network and displayed at the McCormick Place, Chicago, Illinois, on June 8, 2003.

Ashrita Furman balanced 81 pint (20-ounce) glasses on his chin for 12.10 seconds in his backyard in Jamaica, New York. This incredible balancing act, which he performed on August 12, 2007, secured him the record for **most pint glasses balanced on the chin**!

The **longest duration balancing in box splits between two objects** is 12 minutes, 44 seconds and was achieved by Syed Marij Hussain of Pakistan at Punjab Youth Festival 2014 in Lahore, Pakistan, on February 28, 2014. This more than tripled the duration of the last record.

RIGHT ON THE NOSE!
The **most hot-water bottles burst with the nose in one minute** is . . . three! These hot-water bottles were burst by Jemal Tkeshelashvili of the Republic of Georgia, during a live broadcast in Germany on June 2, 2012.

Building a house of cards is fun, but it usually falls down before it gets more than a foot tall. Take a look at the **tallest house of cards**, though—this soaring skyscraper is more than 25 feet, 9 inches tall! It was built on October 16, 2007, by Bryan Berg in Dallas, Texas.

The **fastest crocheter** is Lisa Gentry, who crocheted a total of 5,113 stitches in 30 minutes at the Michaels Arts and Crafts Store, Monroe, Louisiana. She stitched her way to a Guinness World Records title on June 25, 2005.

How many socks can a person wear on one foot? Want to guess? 10? 20? Try 152! Fiona Nolan of Ireland wore 152 socks on March 25, 2011, giving her the record for **most socks worn on one foot simultaneously**.

The **longest time for three people to stay in a box** is 6 minutes, 13.52 seconds. The trio who set this world record were all contortionists and also happen to be related! Sisters Skye Broberg, Nele Siezen, and Jola Siezen from New Zealand squeezed themselves into the box on September 20, 2009.

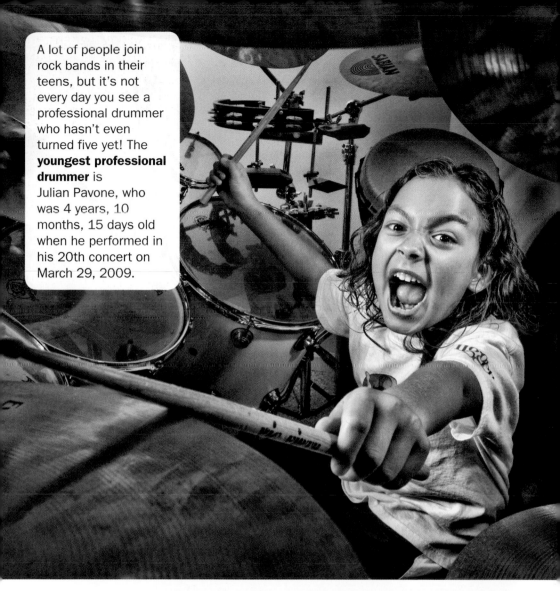

A lot of people join rock bands in their teens, but it's not every day you see a professional drummer who hasn't even turned five yet! The **youngest professional drummer** is Julian Pavone, who was 4 years, 10 months, 15 days old when he performed in his 20th concert on March 29, 2009.

There isn't much point in a cannon that's only 1.25 inches long . . . except to achieve a world record! The **smallest working cannon** is 0.86 of an inch wide and 0.62 of an inch high. This tiny weapon was made by Joseph Brooks and fired in Okeechobee, Florida, on October 22, 2006.

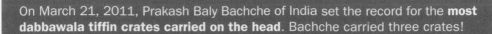

On March 21, 2011, Prakash Baly Bachche of India set the record for the **most dabbawala tiffin crates carried on the head**. Bachche carried three crates!

FACT!
Dabbawalas are people who deliver lunch to offices on long trays that they balance on their heads. Each tray is a tiffin crate—tiffin means "lunch." Dabbawalas are known for their speed as well as for always being on time.

CRAWLING AT THE SPEED OF LIGHT!
Crawling is usually something you do really slowly, but on January 23, 2007, Suresh Joachim crawled one mile in 23 minutes, 45 seconds. He achieved the **fastest mile crawling** in Toronto, Canada.

MORE FUN THAN A . . .

The **longest Barrel of Monkeys chain** is 1,143 feet long and consisted of 5,990 monkeys! This crazy chain of plastic monkeys was strung together by Parker Phinney. It was created and measured in Hanover, New Hampshire, on May 13, 2012.

The world's **largest roll of toilet paper** was 9 feet, 8.9 inches in diameter. That means it was way wider than a human being! This righteous roll was created by Charmin in Cincinnati, Ohio, on August 26, 2011.

The **largest game of head, shoulders, knees, and toes at different places** was played by 4,727 participants! This game took place at 45 locations across the UK on March 1, 2011, at exactly 11:00 a.m.

Haunted houses are scary, but at least they don't usually take too long from start to finish. The **longest walk-through horror house** is the 4,951-feet-long Factory of Terror haunted house located in Canton, Ohio, as verified on September 17, 2014.

The **fastest time to push an orange a distance of one mile using the nose** is 22 minutes, 41 seconds. This wacky record was set by—who else?— Ashrita Furman, on November 2, 2007.

James Devine of Ireland holds the record for **fastest tap dance**. On May 25, 1998, he tapped 38 taps per second! That record hasn't been beaten in 17 years!

DON'T BURST MY BALLOON!
The **most giant balloons entered by a person and burst in two minutes** . . . is 11! This wacky record was set by Paolo Scannavino of Italy, on March 31, 2012.

The **largest pop-up book** was 13 feet, 1 inch by 9 feet, 10 inches when closed. The book, titled *My Word,* was completed on September 6, 2010, for a television commercial by Pearle Opticiens in Belgium.

ALL THE NEWS THAT'S FIT TO PRINT!

The **smallest newspaper** is an edition of the Portuguese newspaper *Terra Nostra*. This teeny-tiny tabloid measured just 0.72 by 0.99 inches and was created by Nova Gráfica on February 16, 2012. The small newspaper, which weighed just 0.04 ounces, was an exact replica of the normal edition, and a total of 3,000 copies went on sale.

Shearing a sheep is like giving someone a haircut . . . if that someone is woolly, wild, and won't stop squirming! It takes a while to get a single sheep sheared. But Hilton Barrett of Australia sheared a sheep in 39.31 seconds flat on May 1, 2010, shaving more than six seconds off the existing record when he achieved the **fastest time to shear one sheep**!

Ilker Yilmaz of Turkey squirted milk from his eye a distance of 9 feet, 2 inches at the Armada Hotel, Istanbul, Turkey, on September 1, 2004. This awesome accomplishment secured him the record for **farthest distance squirting milk**!

Sean Shannon of Canada recited Hamlet's soliloquy "to be or not to be" (which is 260 words) in a time of 23.8 seconds on August 30, 1995. Rattling out his lines at a rate of 655 words per minute, that makes him the **fastest talker**!

SPOONING AROUND!
Have you ever tried to balance a spoon on your elbow or nose? How about your elbow *and* your nose? And your ears, and your cheeks, and your knees and your shoulders and your fingers? The **most spoons balanced on the body** is 52! All the cutlery was balanced on the body of Eitibar Elchiev of the republic of Georgia, on December 7, 2012.

How fast can *you* bend a 20-foot-long iron bar so it fits into a suitcase? Probably not as fast as Alexander Muromskiy of Russia, who did it in 25 seconds! On November 9, 2008, his iron will earned him the title for **fastest iron bar bending to fit into a suitcase**.

Shobha S. Tipnis of India holds the female record for the **fastest time to blow up a hot-water bottle until it bursts**. It took her a mere 41.2 seconds to burst that bottle! Tipnis set this record on the TV show *Guinness World Records—Ab India Todega* in Mumbai, India, on March 17, 2011.

The world's **largest jigsaw puzzle** measured 58,435.1 square feet, and had 21,600 pieces. Created by Great East Asia Surveyors & Consultants Co. Ltd, it was assembled by 777 people in Hong Kong on November 3, 2002.

LET IT SHINE!
The **most shoes shined in eight hours** is 210 pairs. Kieran Porter set this record on behalf of Street Kids International, in London, UK, on April 12, 2012.

Why would anyone want to drink ketchup? To set a world record, of course! In 2012, TV reporter Benedikt Weber drank a 14-ounce bottle of ketchup in 32.37 seconds through a straw—the **fastest time to drink a bottle of ketchup**. He performed the feat on the television show *Galileo* in Germany.

From April 22 to 23, 1998, Ashrita Furman traveled the **greatest distance walked with a milk bottle balanced on the head**: 80.96 miles! The walk lasted for 23 hours, 35 minutes.

The Guinness World Records title for the **most consecutive generations of twins** is shared by two families.

Within the Rollings family of the UK, there have been four consecutive generations of twins born from 1916 to 2002. The first were Elizabeth and Olga Rollings (born December 3, 1916). The second generation saw Margaret and Maureen Hammond (born July 20, 1950). Margaret and Maureen were nieces to Elizabeth and Olga Rollings. The third-generation twins were Fay and Fiona O'Connor (born February 26, 1977). Fay and Fiona were nieces to Margaret and Maureen. And finally, on January 12, 2002, Kacie and Jessica Fawcett were born. They are nieces to Fay and Fiona.

The other record holder is the Taylor family of the USA (pictured). Within the Taylor clan, there have been four consecutive generations of twins born from 1919 to 2002. The first were Gail and Dale Ritchie Taylor (October 19, 1919). The second generation saw Janet and Joyce Taylor (February 5, 1955). The third generation of twins were Debra and Daniel Haroldsen (September 4, 1981). And finally on May 19, 2002, Nathan and Alexander Bartholoma were born.

Nick Janson of the UK has escaped from handcuffs locked on him by more than 1,760 different police officers around the world since 1954. He holds the record for **most handcuff escapes**!

The record for the **fastest tiddlywinks mile** belongs to Ashrita Furman! He managed a mile in 23 minutes, 22 seconds in the Dominican Republic, on December 17, 2007.

Just imagine trying to talk with your mouth full of 400 straws! On August 6, 2009, Simon Elmore from the UK managed to stuff 400 straws into his mouth. He set the record for **most straws stuffed in the mouth** while filming a television show in Bavaria, Germany. Table manners are the last thing on this guy's mind, at least when it comes to record-breaking!

How many people can you fit in *your* car? How about in one of those tiny little Smart cars? The world record for **most people crammed in a Smart car** has two record holders—each group fit 20 people in a Smart car! This epic squeeze was accomplished by the Glendale Cheerleading Team (pictured) on the set of *Guinness World Records Gone Wild* at the Staples Center in Los Angeles on September 28, 2011, and then equaled by the Comets Cheerleaders on the set of *Lo Show dei Record* in Milan, Italy, on July 3, 2014.

Usually advertisements are supposed to be as big as possible—but this ad was made as tiny as possible! It's the **smallest advertisement** in the world, and it measures only 65.15 by 59.34 micrometers. This puny promo was created by Gillette—Procter & Gamble at the University of Nottingham's Nanotechnology and Nanoscience Centre, UK, on April 14, 2011.

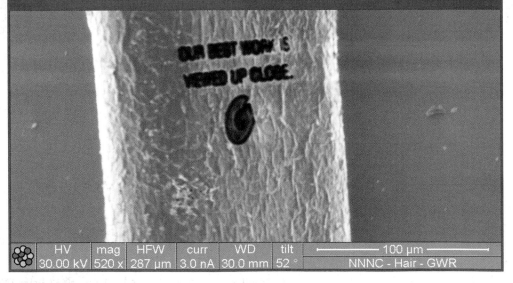

	HV	mag	HFW	curr	WD	tilt	100 μm
	30.00 kV	520 x	287 μm	3.0 nA	30.0 mm	52 °	NNNC - Hair - GWR

ALL WASHED OUT!

The world's **smallest washing machine** measures just 10.08 by 10.94 inches by 1 foot, 3.04 inches. This tiny washer was made by Qingdao Haier Washing Machine Co, Ltd. of China and was unveiled in Qingdao City, Shandong Province, China, on May 18, 2011. The washing machine weighs 11 pounds, 12 ounces and has a tiny washing capacity of just 5.29 ounces.

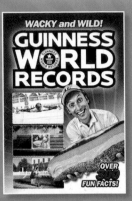
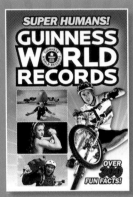

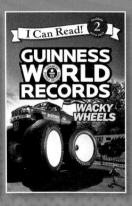